# THE 4 BIGGEST MISTAKES TRADES PEOPLE ARE MAKING WITH THEIR WEBSITES...

## and how YOU can avoid them!

by Rick. P. Nielsen

# MOTIVATION

*"for those about to rock, we salute you"*
*AC/DC*

# DEDICATION

*to all the trades people who struggle each day to make their dreams come true...this one is for you.*

# TABLE OF CONTENTS

# CHAPTER 1
## INTRODUCTION

by Rick.P. Nielsen

Way back in 1986, the great Phil Collins released a song titled "Land of Confusion". It was a smash hit back in the day. (The MTV video, on the other hand, always creeped me out!)

Anyway, little did Mr. Collins know he had written the theme song for the up-and-coming "World Wide Web"! Talk about a Land of Confusion!

And who is the biggest culprit of all this confusion? WEBSITES!! YES! Those damn websites!!

On any given day, there are THOUSANDS of companies across the globe offering up some version of their "World Class Website Super Product" and "Unmatched Services" ...blah, blah, blah.

Did I mention **THOUSANDS**??

Ok. It is bad enough that the lingo in this industry is littered with acronyms: SEO, SEM, FTP, SMTP, POP, IMAP, HTML and on and on and on and on and on. It's like they were too lazy to spell anything out...and I thought I was bad!

This is where the confusion comes in. SO much of how websites are sold to businesses, especially the trades industry is based on, you guessed it, confusion. It's a wonder anyone can get a website up and running!

Whether intentional or not, all this tech-speak gobbledygook littering the web can put most business owners in a weird Zombie like state. Having no clue what to do, many business owners end up choosing a website provider as if they are throwing a dart aimlessly at a dart board.

Let me put it another way. Say your spouse sends you to the grocery store to pick up some olive oil (don't brag about that to your friends, BTW). You arrive at the isle that stocks the olive oil only to discover it runs the ENTIRE 100 feet of isle. From the top of the shelf to the bottom. You stand there, a hazy, confused glare begins to loom over your eyes as you gaze aimlessly into the olive oil abyss.

And with no clear instructions on what olive oil to buy, you close your eyes, grab the first one you can and dart out. Hoping to God you chose the one that will not require another painful trip back to the store.

Ya...we have all been there.

Well, that is EXACTLY what it's like trying to sift thought the world of website providers.

But that ends for you TODAY...right here, right now!

You see, I wrote this book with the intention of opening your eyes to this "Land of Confusion" and hopefully it will make things less confusing.

Now, this book is not intended to make you into some super Ninja webmaster. Not in the slightest. It is, however, designed to give you the basic building blocks needed in order to have a highly effective and income producing website.

So, with that out of way, let's get started!

Oh, I guess maybe I should let you in on who I am. **DUH!!**

My name is Rick Nielsen. (and no, not the lead guitarist for band Cheap Trick)

I have been an Internet web professional for the last 22 years. I have run 3 successful web agencies over those 22 years, building and hosting websites for small mom and pop shops all the way up to Fortune 500 companies.

I have personally built over 800 websites and provide consulting and guidance to over 1000 more companies.

In the last 12 months, however, I have switched my attention to working exclusively with individuals and businesses within the trades industry.

Why you ask? Well, growing up, my dad, who is still hammering away at 82, is highly skilled carpenter. And from the ages age 8 to 23, I worked with him on hundreds of job sites.

Once I moved to the web as my full-time occupation, I remained friends with dozens of people within the trades industry. And I began to see something very disheartening.

I noticed how many of them struggled to get consistent business. They had lost significant amounts of money trying to get a nice website put together. And worst of all, I seen how shady-ass companies used the "Land of Confusion" to take advantage of them.

So that brings me to today. I created The Trades Person Organization to help bring clarity to this "Land of Confusion". I provide killer mobile sites, marketing and operational training to those tired and weary of getting only mediocre results.

There, now ya know! So, let's move forward. Shall we??

Buckle up kids, this is going to be a bumpy ride!

Rick Nielsen

# WEBSITE FACT #1

*The first web page came online in 1992. It was published by Tim Berners-Lee. The web address is:*

*http://info.cern.ch/hypertext/WWW/TheProject.html*

Wow, we have come along way!

# CHAPTER 2
## NO CALL TO ACTION

by Rick.P. Nielsen

Now I'm sure you've heard the phrase, "Call to Action" before. It has been around the advertising world for years.

In a nutshell, a call to action is a phrase used to instruct potential customers what to do when they see an ad. They are heavily used on many TV commercials and nearly all infomercials. "Call Now" or "Order Now" are the two-best known to the average TV viewer (but wait, there's more).

In fact, I think my mom invented the call to action. It went something like this: "Get off your ass and clean your room!" or "Stop picking on your sister right his very minute!!" or my favorite "Stop picking your nose or your head will cave in!" (my mom should have worked at an ad agency). And when she said it, you knew EXACTLY what to do! It was, to say the least, clear and concise!!!

Same goes for your website.

You see, your website is nothing more than a digital tool. Its sole purpose is to take a website visitor and "convert" them into a potential customer. Either by calling you, dropping by your place of business or filling out a web form.

But here's the thing.

VERY FEW WEBSITES HAVE A CALL TO ACTION!

Why you ask?

Well, believe it or not, most "web designers" know very little about marketing. Thus, the web sites they design end up becoming very fancy, over bloated brochure sites. And that, my friend does absolutely NOTHING to increase your bottom line.

And a hefty bottom line is what I believe most web site owners want (but hey, I've been wrong before... just not in this case).

To make this simple, here are the two things needed to activate your websites "Customer Getting Superpowers":

1. Simple and clear call to action on the home page.

2. Place that call to action "Above the Fold" on your web site (Above the Fold is old newspaper ad lingo used to describe where to place important front-page stories).

In the digital world, above the fold means the call to action needs to be visible on the screen as soon as a visitor hits a website. There should be zero scrolling to see it. It needs to be... BOOM! Right there, on the screen with clear instruction on what to do next.

Let's check out a powerful "**Call To Action**" example on the next page, shall we???

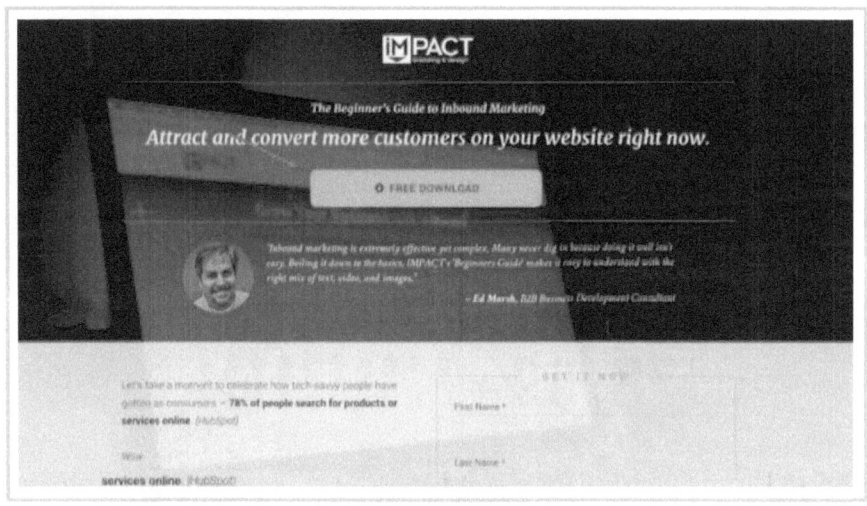

**Web Page A**

Take note of the button text in this example:
**"FREE DOWNLOAD"**

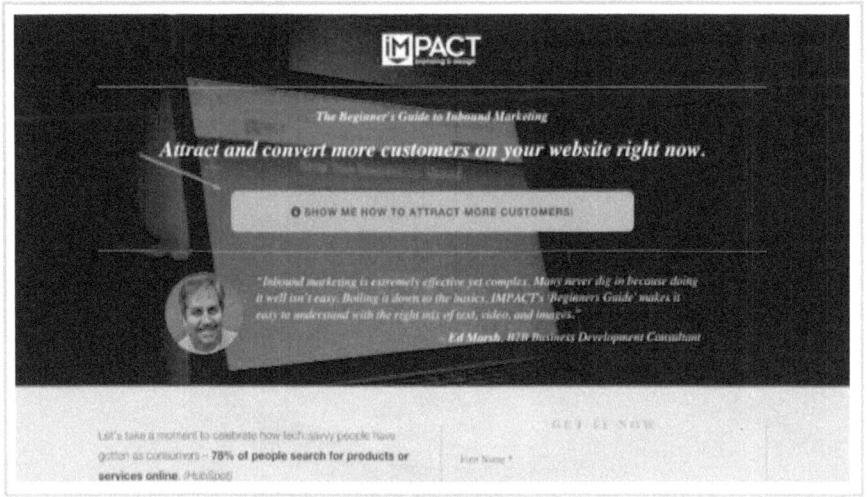

**Web Page B**

Now, look at the button text in this example:
**"SHOW ME HOW TO ATTRACT MORE CUSTOMERS"**

Now, you wouldn't think such a small difference in the call to action would make any significant difference in the results.

Oh...but it did. And in a BIG way! With only a slight wording change on the button, Example B increased the company's conversion rate to... wait for it...

# 78.5% !!!!!!!!!!!

And that my friend is how you turn an ordinary website into an extra ordinary website!

(*insert mic drop here, exit stage left*)

Never forget this: words do matter. Especially on the web. And a strong, well thought-out call to action can change your business almost overnight.

Make sure your site has a great Call to Action!

Here ends the lesson...

# WEBSITE FACT #2

*As of January 2020, there were over 1.74 billion websites on the Internet as of August 2020.*

# CHAPTER 3
## DOING IT YOURSELF

Over the course of my twenty plus years as a web marketer/ designer, I've had the privilege of working with over a 1000 clients. In that same timeframe, I have talked with thousands more.  And I can say with no uncertainty that at least three-fourths of them have attempted to build a website on their own.

As small business owners, we are wired to try and do as much ourselves as we can. Or near most everything.

And I get that. I'm as guilty as anyone else!

But early on in my career, it became painstakingly obvious that somethings needed to be handled by professionals if I wanted to see ANY growth and success in my business.

One reason so many business owners attempt the "I will build my own website" stunt is because they don't understand the true value a client-gathering website can be (discussed in the previous chapter).

Let me put it this way.

How many times have you been hired for a project, only to find out the customer attempted to do it themselves? They tell you they watched HGTV, a few YouTube videos and had a "Hold my beer and watch this" moment. Only to discover it was WAY more difficult than they had ever imagined.

And how did that project go?

More than likely, you had to go in and redo everything because they screwed it all up. My dad is famous for saying that "It's going to take longer to undo what they did just to get it right"!

I'm guessing that is true for you as well.

Bottom line is this. People call you because YOU are the professional. You are the expert in your field. And, at the end of the day, they want the job done right.

So why would you try to build a website yourself without any of the skill sets needed to do so? Do what your customers do! Hire someone who is a professional and knows how they can turn your website from shabby chic to a client gathering monster!

As with your profession, becoming a web professional takes year, even decades of consistent hard work to become skilled at it. Unless you actually get PAID to build websites, it is a task reserved for those as skilled at it as you are with your trade.

In the grand scheme of things, the cost of a website is irrelevant compared to the returns that you will receive, if done properly. You can only get that, however, from someone that is a veteran in the web profession. And I'm not talking about a web designer. There are great web designers out there, but that doesn't mean they are skilled MARKETERS. You need someone who is in the web field that is first and foremost, marketing driven.

If you're going to see any sort of return on your website investment, it can't just be a pretty brochure site. It needs to be designed and engineered to do one thing and one thing only. Convert visitors into potential customers by contacting you.

That's it. No more, no less.

Look, I'm not downplaying people getting into the web design industry. I too was a rookie and didn't know what the hell I was doing most of time. But being a web and marketing professional has been all I have done over the last 22 years, so, needless to say, I've seen a few things.

Let the newbies and rookies take on other clients to hone their skills. Don't let them use you as their learning platform. If you're looking to move your business to the next level, get the best customers for your business and transform your business from an also-ran into an empire, you need to have a seasoned web veteran in your corner. Then and only then will you be able to see the return on investment you made into your new mobile friendly website.

# CHAPTER 4
## NOT MOBILE FRIENDLY

Now this is a big one baby. In fact, this one thing alone, if done right, could completely change the direction of your business for the good. So, let's talk numbers.

"In the USA, 94% of people with smartphones search for local information on their phones. Interestingly, 77% of mobile searches occur at home or at work, places where desktop computers are likely to be present."

"Nearly half of mobile users switch to your competitor instead, after a bad experience with your mobile site."

"57% of consumers said: A business with a poorly designed mobile website is not likely to be recommended."

"Load Speed: 5 seconds or less, guarantee 70% longer viewing sessions."

"Google might now eliminate your webpage from rankings in a mobile search (SERPs) if your webpage is not mobile-friendly."

"9 out of 10 customers are lost due to a lower mobile-friendly experience."

"More than half of mobile consumers who are let down by a mobile version of a website think negative about the business itself."

Here is a clip from Google's Webmaster Blog:

## Google Webmaster Central Blog

Official news on crawling and indexing sites for the Google index

### Announcing mobile first indexing for the whole web

Thursday, March 05, 2020

It's been a few years now that Google started working on mobile-first indexing - Google's crawling of the web using a smartphone Googlebot. From our analysis, most sites shown in search results are good to go for mobile-first indexing, and 70% of those shown in our search results have already shifted over. To simplify, we'll be switching to mobile-first indexing for all websites starting September 2020. In the meantime, we'll continue moving sites to mobile-first indexing when our systems recognize that they're ready.

Let me highlight the main sentence in this blog post:

*"**To simplify, we'll be switching to mobile-first indexing for all websites staring September 2020.**"*

In layman's terms, here is what Google is saying. If your website is not mobile friendly, your ranking will be pushed down below every and all mobile-friendly sites, regardless of any work you have previously done to improve your rank! How's that for a kick in the head??

by Rick.P. Nielsen

Continuing on, if a picture is worth a thousand words, then the following example is worth **thousands of dollars** to you and your bank account. Look over each example closely.

There is a short quiz on the next page!

**Mobile Site A**          **Mobile Site B**

Now, no one can guarantee you results in terms of how you can rank in search engines. **NO ONE!** Not even me. And anyone who does guarantee you a specific result is, well, a big fat liar!

You see, Google's crazy-ass algorithm is a mystery to everyone. They only tell us part of what it takes to rank a site. It's impossible to win a game when the rules are guarded as tightly as

Google's algorithm.

You can, however, do everything in your power to implement the rules you DO know. It can greatly increase your odds of getting a higher ranking. And having a killer mobile-friendly website is the main key needed to increase your odds.

# OK. QUIZ TIME!

So, for your benefit only, please answer the following questions HONESTLY! Not with your business/ego hat. But rather, with your commonsense hat. Ready? Here we go!!

1.Using the same search term, which site do you think will rank higher? **A** or **B**
2. Which website is easier to read on a phone? **A** or **B**
3. Which website do you think you are more likely to visit on a mobile phone? **A** or **B**
4. Which site makes it easier to contact them from a mobile phone? **A** or **B**

If you answered **B** to all four questions, you now possess the knowledge needed to make a change!

I tell all my clients: "You can't **DO** what is possible till you first **KNOW** what is possible. Well, now you know what is possible, so what are **YOU** going to do about it?

# WEBSITE FACT #3

*every day slightly more than 547,200 new websites are created globally.*

# CHAPTER 5
## NOT A PRIORITY

by Rick.P. Nielsen

As an entrepreneur, you are constantly on the move. Taking care of clients, working diligently on projects for those clients, ordering materials, dealing with employees, chasing down money, etc. And that's just for work!

Pile on the non-stop responsibilities at home and it's a wonder you ever had time to really sit down and think about a website, let alone one that can actually produce results.

Look, most trades people know they NEED a website. But many haven't grasped the true power a great website can be. But hey, that's not your fault! How could you know? It's not your skill set!

Believe it or not, your website is the center of your entire advertising, marketing and business universe. It is your only 24 hour a day, 7 day a week, 365 day a year employee that never fails to get the job done.

In most cases, your website is the first impression your potential customers will have with you and your business. Does it represent you well? Does it show that you are on top of your game? Or, does it fall short?

Here's the thing. You may be the most skilled handyman, plumber, roofer or HVAC person in your field. But, if your website is outdated, hard to read on mobile and lacks an easy way for potential customers to reach you, they will never find out how good you are. They will simply "click" to the next listing on

Google and contact someone else. It is the equivalent of throwing thousands of dollars into the trash.

TODAY is the day to move your website to the top of your "to-do" list and turn it into the number one money making tool in your toolbox!

# WEBSITE FACT #4

*It takes about 50 milliseconds (that's 0.05 seconds) for users to form an opinion about your website that determines whether they like your site or not, whether they'll stay or leave.*

# CHAPTER 6
## CONCLUSION

As I mentioned in the beginning of this book, my intentions were not to try and turn you into some wiz-bang web expert. Rather, I simply wanted to make you fully aware of how, with just a few simple but powerful ideas, transform your website into the customer gathering machine it should be!

Over the course of my career, I've seen far too many business owners fall into the "Seduction by Fads" trap. What I have covered here for you today is anything but a 'Fad".

These are the fundamentals that have been time-tested, in the trenches, with real businesses getting real results.

Someone once told me that not knowing something is one of the most dangerous aspects of business. Not knowing can cost you money, erode valuable time and damage your reputation.

By reading and ACTING on the information within the pages of this book, it can position you with an enormous and completive advantage over anyone else in you field.

Now, if you found anything in this book to be helpful in anyway, and you are actively and ambitiously searching for more, I may have just what you're looking for!

I have put together a short but powerful FREE VIDEO for those looking for a success breakthrough using the power of a mobile websites.

In this video, I will cover, in more detail, the why's and how's of getting a new, client attracting website. I will demo an example website and cover, in painstaking detail, how to become one of the few trades people who are puised and ready for a success hreakthrough!

So, if you're ready to transform your business, please see the next page!

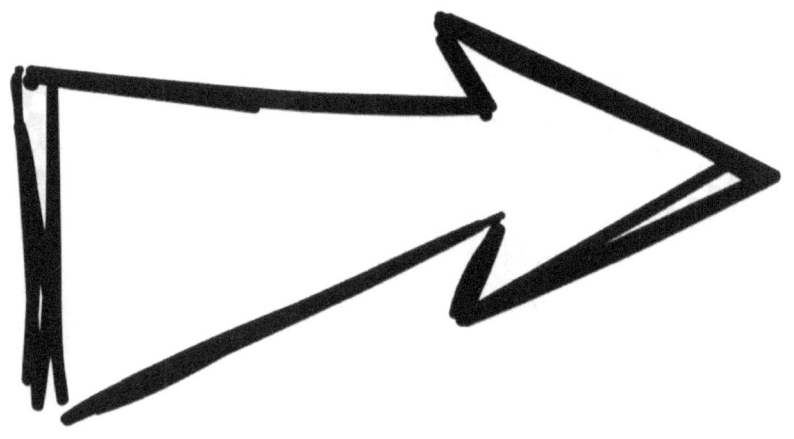

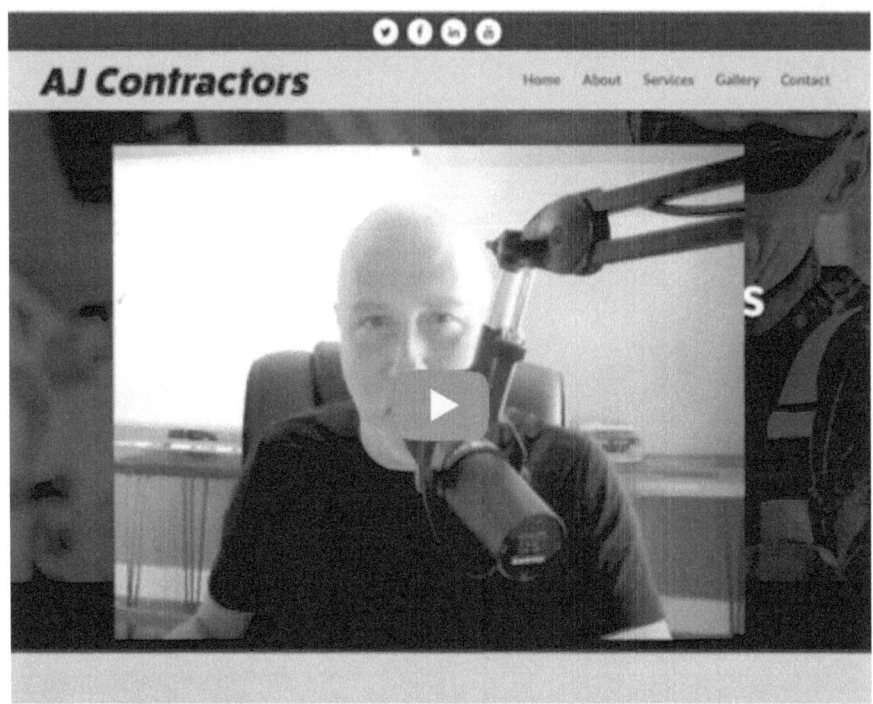

To get access to this COMPLEMENTARY VIDEO, simply visit:

## https://thetradesperson.com/video-01.html

Now, you will find NO sales pitch and NO high-pressure sales tactics. Instead, just the why's and the how's. If you like what you see, take the next step. If not, I hope you were able to learn something that can make your current website even more effective!

Thanks for taking the time to read this book and I hope to see you on the other side.

## Example A: Mobile Friendly Contrator Site

https://site1.thetradesperson.com


## Example B: Mobile Friendly Plumber Site

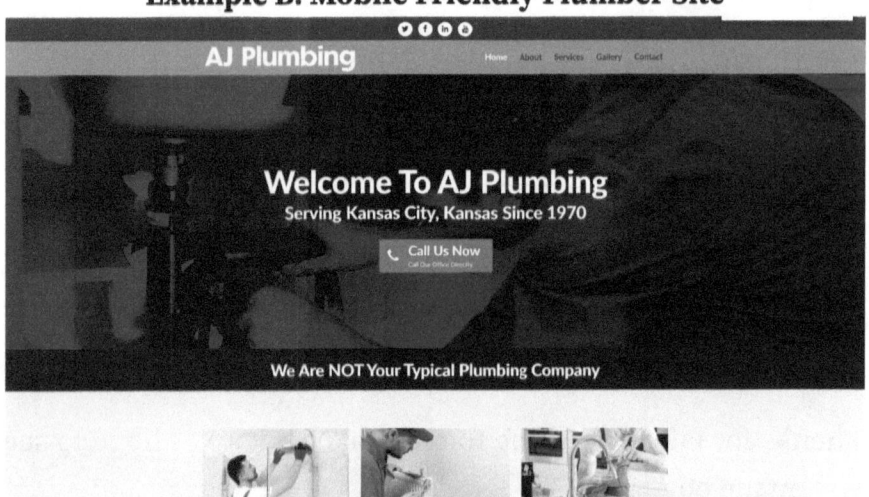

https://site2.thetradesperson.com